ENDANGERED!

SHARKS

Amanda Harman

Series Consultant: James G. Doherty
General Curator, The Bronx Zoo, New York

BENCHMARK BOOKS

MARSHALL CAVENDISH
NEW YORK

Benchmark Books
Marshall Cavendish Corporation
99 White Plains Road
Tarrytown, New York 10591-9001

Library of Congress Cataloging-in-Publication Data

Harman, Amanda. 1968-
   Sharks / by Amanda Harman.
      p.   cm. — (Endangered!)
   Includes bibliographical references (p.   ).
   Summary: Discusses the three biggest species of sharks, all of
which may be in danger of disappearing because people hunt them for
profit and fish them for sport.
   ISBN 0-7614-0220-9 (lib. bdg.)
   1. White shark—Juvenile literature.   2. Whale shark—Juvenile
literature.   3. Basking shark—Juvenile literature.   4. Sharks—
Juvenile literature.   5. Endangered species—Juvenile literature.
[1. White shark. 2. Whale shark. 3. Basking shark. 4. Sharks.
5. Endangered species.]   I. Title. II. Series.
QL638.9.H36 1996
597'.31—dc20   95-48170
                                                CIP
                                                  AC

Printed in Hong Kong

PICTURE CREDITS

*The publishers would like to thank the following for supplying the photographs
used in this book:* Ardea 10, 12, 15, 16, 20, 23, 29; Bruce Coleman Ltd 1, 8,
14, 17, 19, 21, 22, 24; Frank Lane Picture Agency (FLPA) 6, 28;
Earthviews/FLPA 11; Walt Clayton/Earthviews/FLPA 13; Bob
Commer/Earthviews/FLPA 5; Panda/FLPA FC, 4, 7, 18, 26.

Series created by Brown Packaging

Front cover: Great white shark.
Title page: Great white shark.
Back cover: Whale shark.

DATE DUE

APR 2 ? 3

OCT 25

MAR 0 3 2001

Contents

Introduction

Chances are, if you were asked to picture a shark, you would think of a ferocious, man-eating animal. Or maybe you would imagine a pointed, triangular fin cutting menacingly through the surface of the water. But there are about 350 **species** of sharks in the world, and they come in many shapes and sizes.

Some sharks, such as the various reef sharks and the blue shark, look pretty much as you may have imagined. They are beautifully streamlined hunters with pointed snouts and mouths full of sharp teeth. Others, though, look

The Caribbean reef shark has the typical shape of a shark. It lives on coral reefs and can be dangerous to people.

very different. A hammerhead, for example, really does have a head shaped like a hammer. And some sharks are not even hunters but swim along feeding on tiny animals called **plankton**. A very small number of sharks, like the whale shark, are enormous, but over half the species never grow to more than 39 inches (1 m) in length. The average size is about five feet (1.5 m) long.

Because not all species of sharks eat the same food, they have different kinds of teeth. Tiger sharks, which will eat almost anything, have large, broad, jagged teeth. Others, like sand tiger sharks, feed mostly on fish. These sharks have long, thin teeth that can grip the slippery, wriggling bodies of their **prey**. Horn sharks have teeth at the back of their mouth that are shaped like flat plates and are used for crushing the shells of clams and crabs.

Hammerhead sharks are hunting sharks. Some scientists think that the shape of their head makes them more agile in the water. These sharks' eyes are at each side of the "hammer."

Introduction

Not all sharks swim near the surface of the sea. Some, like the megamouth shark, swim in the dark ocean depths, while others, such as the wobbegongs, live on the seabed. These bottom-dwelling sharks usually have flattened undersides that allow them to lie on the sea floor, and their backs are often colored and patterned to help them blend in with the sand and rocks.

Sharks are fish. Like other fish, they have **gills** for breathing instead of lungs. Unlike that of most other fish, however, a shark's skeleton is made not of bone but of a tough, flexible material called **cartilage**. The only other fish to have a cartilage skeleton are the sharks' closest relatives, the rays, ratfish, and skates. All the rest are "bony" fish.

A sand tiger shark, a fish-eater, shows off its long, sharp teeth. Sand tigers are usually about 8 feet 6 inches (2.6 m) in length and can be found in many seas.

Sharks have swum in the oceans for millions of years, and during that time some species have become **extinct**. They could not **adapt** to changes in their environment. Today, the three biggest species of sharks may also be in danger of disappearing because people hunt them for profit or fish them for sport. In this book, we are going to look at these large species – first of all, the great white shark, and then the whale shark and the basking shark.

A horn shark makes its way across the sea floor. Its markings make it hard to see among the rocks.

Great White Shark

This is the tiger of the seas and the largest of the hunting sharks. Great whites can reach more than 20 feet (6 m) from head to tail and weigh over 7000 pounds (3200 kg). Females are generally larger than males, and some scientists believe that male great whites change into females if they reach a certain size. No one knows exactly why this may happen. The reason might be that a large, strong shark has a better chance of giving birth to healthy babies than a small, weak one does.

The great white shark's body is shaped like a torpedo. It has a slightly pointed, cone-shaped snout, and becomes wider just before the middle part of the body and then

A great white shark moves silently just below the surface. The great white belongs to a group of heavy-set but fast sharks called mackerel sharks.

8

tapers to a thin, crescent-shaped tail. This gives it a very streamlined shape, which means that the fish can cruise for a long time without tiring. It has three main fins, two sticking out from the sides of its body and one on its back. The two side fins are called pectoral fins, and the one on its back is called the dorsal fin. It is this fin that shows above the water when a shark is swimming close to the surface. In the case of the great white, the tail may show as well.

Despite its name, the great white shark is white only on its underside. The top of its head, back, and tail are a gray-brown or charcoal color. Like that of other sharks, the great white's skin is covered with tiny toothlike scales. Unlike

Areas where the great white shark can be found

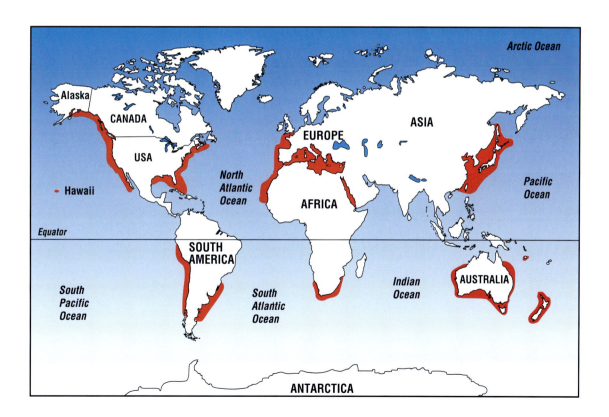

bony fish, sharks and their relatives do not have a swimbladder. This is a special organ that holds gas to keep fish buoyant in the water and prevent them from sinking to the seabed. Instead of a swimbladder, sharks have a large liver full of a kind of oil that weighs much less than the water in which they swim.

Even so, great whites have to swim constantly, otherwise they would fall slowly to the sea floor. Another reason they must keep moving is to keep water passing over their gills so that they can breathe. A great white has to swim at an average speed of 2 miles per hour (3.2 km/h) every minute of the day, otherwise it will drown!

The great white's dark back makes it harder to spot from above. This helps the shark approach its prey from below without being seen.

The great white shark is a fearsome **predator**. There is a long list of creatures that it will eat, including squid, crabs, sea turtles, fish such as tuna and swordfish, and other sharks. But its favorite prey are sea-dwelling **mammals**, such as seals, dolphins, porpoises, and sea lions. It will also feed on **carrion**, such as dead seabirds and whales, which it finds floating in the water.

The great white is one of the few sharks that hunt and feed on mammals. To be able to do so it needs several special **adaptations**. One of these adaptations is an amazing sense of smell, which probably allows the shark to detect one drop of blood in about 25 gallons (100 liters) of water! Great whites have a habit of coming to the surface and poking their heads out of the water. Recent scientific

A great white on the lookout for food. Though these sharks swim fairly slowly most of the time, they can move at great speeds – perhaps 20 miles per hour (32 km/h) – when they need to.

studies seem to show that the great white may do this in order to sniff the air with the nostrils on its snout. However, great whites also have excellent eyesight, so they might be looking for prey rather than trying to smell it. Whatever the reason, great whites are the only sharks that are known to thrust their heads out of the water in this way.

As well as wonderful eyesight and a fantastic sense of smell, the great white has two other ways of finding creatures in the water. Running through the shark's head and body is a series of tubes filled with a type of jelly. As fish and other animals swim nearby, the waves they make in the water cause ripples in the jelly that tell the shark

With its huge jaws wide open, a great white prepares to attack. Great whites close their eyes just before they strike in order to protect them.

where they are. Great whites also have special **pores** on their snout. These can pick up tiny electric signals coming from the muscles in the bodies of other sea creatures.

When searching for prey, a great white shark will often patrol in deep water, close to the seabed. Once it has detected a victim, it launches an attack from below. Swimming up rapidly and closing in for the kill, the shark lifts its nose and grabs the animal in its huge, powerful jaws. Sometimes the shark strikes so powerfully that it rises into the air high above the surface of the water, with its catch gripped in its mouth.

As it falls back into the water, the shark rolls over, ripping out a chunk of flesh with its sharp, triangular teeth. Because sharks cannot actually chew their food, the great white has to swallow this lump whole. As it feeds, its huge

A great white pokes its nose above the surface as it feeds. Experts believe that a great white can eat enough food in one meal to last it for two months.

body thrashes in the water as the shark tears out piece after piece until its prey has all been eaten.

The great white shark has teeth with jagged edges like the teeth of a saw. Each tooth is about 3 inches (7.5 cm) long, and each shark has about 3000 of them at a time. They are arranged in many rows, although a great white uses only the first and second rows for feeding. The other rows are there to replace teeth that fall out or break, which may happen every few days. When a tooth is damaged, a replacement simply moves forward to take its place.

At one time, scientists believed that great whites lived alone. However, recent studies have shown that this may

A great white examines a piece of meat put out to bring it close to the camera. These sharks are curious and will check out anything unusual in the area where they live.

The great white shark is one of the top predators in the ocean. Besides people, this magnificent fish has few enemies.

not be true. Biologists off San Francisco tracked two large females (named Trail-Tail and Stumpy by the researchers) who seemed to swim and hunt together regularly.

The biologists also watched several great whites gather in the water below a new kill and compete with one another for food. Most of the time the sharks simply threatened by "hunching" their backs, pointing their fins downward, and opening their jaws wide. However, sometimes the competition ended in violence. Many great whites have scars and pieces of fins or tail missing where they have been bitten by other sharks.

Great White Shark

Very little is known about the great white's breeding behavior. Scientists do know that females give birth to a litter of 2 to 14 live young – rather than eggs – in warm, shallow water. These babies are fully formed great white sharks at birth and measure up to 5 feet 3 inches (1.6 m) long. As soon as the young are born, their mother leaves them to fend for themselves. They feed on fish, including other small sharks.

Also known as "man-eater" or "white death," the great white is the shark that terrifies people most of all. It is true that more people have been killed or injured by great whites than by any other shark, but such attacks are still

A great white bursts through the surface. These powerful animals have been known to leap clear out of the water and into a boat.

very rare. In fact, more people each year are killed in car accidents or by animals such as hippos, elephants, and crocodiles than by great whites.

It also seems that great whites do not really like to eat people. A number of divers have said that great whites have come up to them, had a careful look, and then swum off. Some experts think that the sharks attack only when they mistake people for their usual prey. From below, a person swimming at the surface may look like a seal or sea lion. Great whites have also been known to attack and sink small boats and to shatter surf boards. They probably think the boats and boards are prey or even competitors for food.

Because the great white is so large, many people have hunted and killed this shark for sport. They see it as a huge challenge to reel in such a powerful fish. Commercial

Some tourists want to see great whites and take pictures of them. To bring sharks to the surface, food is left on the end of a line. This shark has just taken the food and can now swim away unharmed.

fishermen also catch great whites along with other species of sharks. Many parts of a shark are useful to people. These include the skin, the teeth and jaws (which are used for ornaments and weapons), and oil from the liver. Also, their fins are used to make "shark fin soup." Fishermen hunting sharks for this purpose cut the fins off and throw the live sharks back into the water to die. This cruel practice is called "finning" and was banned in the United States in 1993 and in Canada in 1994. However, it still continues in other parts of the world.

Altogether, millions of sharks, including great whites, are caught every year. So many great whites have been

The great white uses its tail to push itself through the water, while its fins give it balance. A shark that has been "finned" cannot keep upright and dies.

killed that this shark is probably at risk. Because of this, the great white is now protected along the coasts of California and South Africa, and there are plans to help the shark in Australian waters. In addition, some shark experts hope to change people's attitudes toward this fantastic fish. They are trying to teach people to see the great white not as a savage killing machine but as an intelligent and magnificent marine hunter. They believe that if people understand the shark better they may learn to respect it and leave it alone. People's views on the great white may be changing already in some places. When California decided to protect the shark, it received a lot of public support.

Because great white sharks are so big and dangerous, studying them is not easy. Here divers film a huge great white from inside a shark cage.

Whale & Basking Sharks

The whale shark gets its name from its huge size. At 40 feet (12 m) or more in length and 15 tons in weight, it is as big as some whales and is the largest fish in the world. The whale shark's back and sides are dark gray with yellowish spots and stripes that make the fish look like a giant checkerboard. A whale shark's skin is incredibly thick – in one shark, it was found to measure 4 inches (10 cm).

The whale shark has a broad, flat head, with a rounded snout and tiny eyes. It has two pectoral fins, two dorsal fins, and a tail in which the top fin is much larger than the

A whale shark glides through a sunlit ocean. Each shark has such distinctive markings that researchers can use them to identify individuals.

lower one. The most outstanding feature of this shark, though, is its huge mouth, which may measure up to 4 feet 6 inches (1.4 m) wide. Whale sharks are found in the warm waters on either side of the Equator. They live both along the coast and in the open sea.

The second largest fish in the world is the basking shark, which can weigh up to about 4 tons. Males can reach 30 feet (9 m) and females 32 feet (9.8 m) long. Unlike the whale shark, the basking shark is found only in coastal waters and prefers cooler zones. These two huge fish have much in common, and we will look at them together.

The whale shark and the basking shark are both slow swimmers and do not usually travel any faster than about

A basking shark feeding as it swims. You can tell this shark from the whale shark by its plain gray unmarked color and its much longer, more "shark-like" snout.

3 miles per hour (5 km/h). However, they are completely harmless to people and marine mammals, because they are not meat-eaters. Instead, they feed mainly on plankton – microscopic sea creatures, including tiny shrimplike animals called krill, arrow-worms, fish eggs, and the young of crabs and shrimps. The sharks filter these little creatures from the water, using their huge gills like sieves.

The basking shark feeds by simply swimming through "clouds" of plankton with its mouth wide open, closing it only now and then. When it closes its mouth, the water that it has taken in passes over thick fringes called **gill rakers**. These are made up of thousands of bristles, each about

A basking shark is so big and needs so much energy just to keep moving that it must feed nonstop. Its mouth is so big a child could walk into it without bending down.

4 inches (10 cm) long. The water passes out of the shark through the five gill slits on either side of the shark's neck, but any plankton in the water remains behind. The tiny bodies of the plankton are caught on the gill rakers for the basking shark to swallow. The fish may take in and expel more than 1500 gallons (6000 liters) of seawater in an hour.

The whale shark, on the other hand, can actually suck its prey into its mouth. Because of this, it is able to eat larger prey, such as squid and small fish, which can swim out of the way of basking sharks. It also eats plankton. The whale shark usually feeds as it cruises slowly through the ocean. However, whale sharks have also been seen to feed while

A diver swims above a feeding whale shark. Although whale sharks do not attack people, their scales are sharp and can cause bad cuts.

"hanging" upright in the water. Like the basking shark, the whale shark uses large gill rakers to sieve its food from the tons of seawater that it takes into its mouth. Whale sharks and basking sharks have teeth, but because they do not need them for catching and eating their prey, they are small and of little use.

Both the whale shark and the basking shark spend a lot of time resting in the sunshine, or "basking," at the surface of the ocean, which is how the basking shark got its name. Some fishermen even call it the "sun fish." Basking sharks

A whale shark at the surface. Unlike great whites, whale and basking sharks swim by swinging their whole body – not just the tail – from side to side.

may sunbathe singly, in pairs, in small parties, or even in groups of more than a hundred. Sometimes several basking sharks will swim along slowly near the surface, one behind the other, gently rising and falling in the water as they go. This may be where stories of huge "sea serpents" came from long ago – the back of each shark looked like a curve on the serpent's body as it swam through the sea.

Very little is known about the breeding habits of whale sharks, although it is thought that adults do not become ready to **mate** until they are at least 30 years old! Scientists do know that these sharks lay eggs, since a whale shark egg was once found in the Gulf of Mexico.

Areas where the whale shark can be found

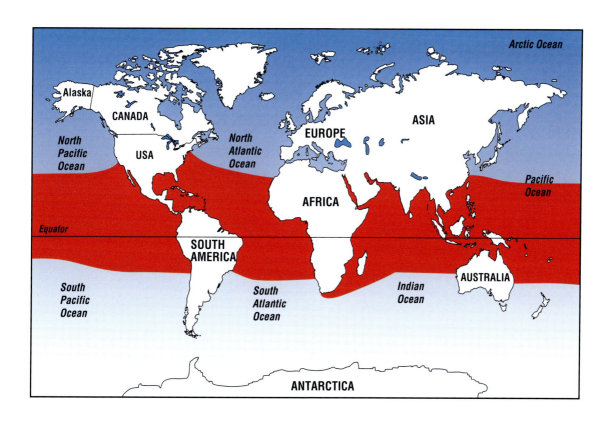

The mouth of the whale shark is right at the front of its head. This is unusual. The mouths of most sharks are beneath the snout on the underside of the head.

A little more is known about the breeding behavior of the basking shark. It is thought that adults become ready to mate when they are between two and four years old. About three and a half years after mating, the female gives birth to one or two live young. Scientists have found that females may have millions of tiny eggs in their bodies. These might be used as food by the baby sharks as they are developing before birth. When they are born, the baby basking sharks are already about 5 feet 6 inches (1.7 m) long – longer than any other sharks at birth, as far as scientists know.

Whale sharks and basking sharks are gentle giants, harmless to humans. In fact, so gentle are they that divers feel perfectly safe swimming alongside them and even riding on their backs. In Australia, whale shark watching is becoming very popular among tourists. Whale sharks seem to be almost as curious as humans and will often swim closer to get a better look at these "strange" creatures who are watching them.

Unfortunately, such a large number of people wanting to see whale sharks up close may be damaging to the sharks and their **habitat**. Rules have been introduced at places such as Ningaloo Reef in Western Australia, where large numbers of whale sharks gather each fall. These state how many people can view sharks at one time and how close they can get to them. Whale shark riding by divers has

Areas where the basking shark can be found

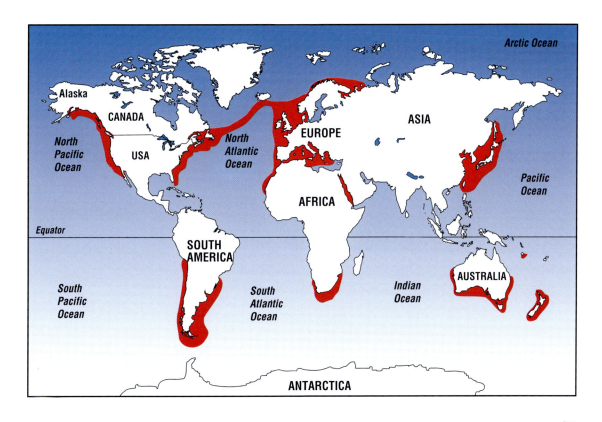

been banned there, too. People are also worried that building too many tourist resorts along the coast may harm the reef for whale sharks and other marine life.

Basking sharks, on the other hand, like great whites, are hunted for their meat and fins. And the liver of a large basking shark can hold hundreds of gallons of oil. The problem is that, like the whale shark, the basking shark is such a mysterious fish that scientists do not know how many there are. Some **conservationists** are worried that fishermen may be taking too many from the sea. They

The body of a basking shark washed up on a beach. It probably died from natural causes since the basking shark has no enemies except people.

would like the hunting of basking sharks to be outlawed until we know more about their numbers.

Because sharks live in the oceans and may travel over huge distances, it is very difficult for researchers to study them or even count them. However, scientists know that the great white shark, the whale shark, and the basking shark are all rare fish. And they are concerned that damage to the marine environment and overfishing may make them – and other kinds of sharks – even more rare. If healthy numbers of sharks are to swim the oceans of the future, fishing for sport and commerce needs to be controlled, and the habitat of these amazing creatures must be conserved.

Scientists believe that whale sharks travel huge distances in search of food. They plan to fit some sharks with radio transmitters so they can track them wherever they go.

Useful Addresses

For more information about sharks and how you can help protect them, contact these organizations:

American Committee for International Conservation
Center for Marine Conservation
1725 DeSales Street NW
Suite 500
Washington, D.C. 20036

The Aquarium for Wildlife Conservation
Surf Avenue & Boardwalk
Brooklyn, New York 11224

Fish & Wildlife Reference Service
5430 Grosvenor Lane
Suite 110
Bethesda, MD 20814

National Wildlife Federation
1400 16th Street NW
Washington, D.C. 20036

U.S. Fish and Wildlife Service
Endangered Species and Habitat
Conservation
400 Arlington Square
18th and C Streets NW
Washington, D.C. 20240

World Wildlife Fund
1250 24th Street NW
Washington, D.C. 20037

Further Reading

Endangered Wildlife of the World (New York: Marshall Cavendish Corporation, 1993)

The Golden Book of Sharks and Whales Kathleen N. Daly (Racine, WI: Western Publishing, 1989)

The Sea World Book of Sharks Eve Bunting (San Diego: Harcourt, 1984)

Shark Michael Chinery (Mahwah, NJ: Troll, 1991)

Shark Miranda MacQuitty (New York: Knopf, 1992)

Sharks! June Behrens (Chicago: Childrens Press, 1990)

Sharks: Challengers of the Deep Mary M. Cervullo (New York: Cobblehill Books, 1993)

Wildlife of the World (New York: Marshall Cavendish Corporation, 1994)

Glossary

Adapt: To change in order to survive in new conditions.

Adaptation: A skill or feature that an animal develops in order to survive.

Carrion (KAR-ee-uhn): Dead animal flesh.

Cartilage: A tough, flexible material that makes up the skeletons of sharks. It is also found around the joints of animals with bony skeletons.

Conservationist (Kon-ser-VAY-shun-ist): A person who protects and preserves the Earth's natural resources, such as animals, plants, and soil.

Extinct (Ex-TINKT): No longer living anywhere in the world.

Gills: The organs through which fish breathe.

Gill rakers: Fringes of bristles found on the gills of whale sharks and basking sharks. Plankton collects on these bristles and is then swallowed by the shark.

Habitat: The place where an animal lives. For example, the basking shark's habitat is cool coastal waters.

Mammal: A kind of animal that is warm-blooded and has a backbone. Most are covered with fur or have hair. Females have glands that produce milk to feed their young.

Mate: When a male and female get together to produce young.

Plankton: The general name for many kinds of tiny plants and animals that live in water, often in huge groups.

Pores: Tiny holes in the skin.

Predator: A kind of animal that hunts and eats other animals.

Prey: An animal that is hunted and eaten by another animal.

Species: A kind of animal or plant. For example, the great white shark is a species of shark.

Index